POWERFUL MEDICINE

BAD BURNS
TRUE SURVIVAL STORIES

SANDRA MARKLE

LERNER PUBLICATIONS COMPANY . MINNEAPOLIS

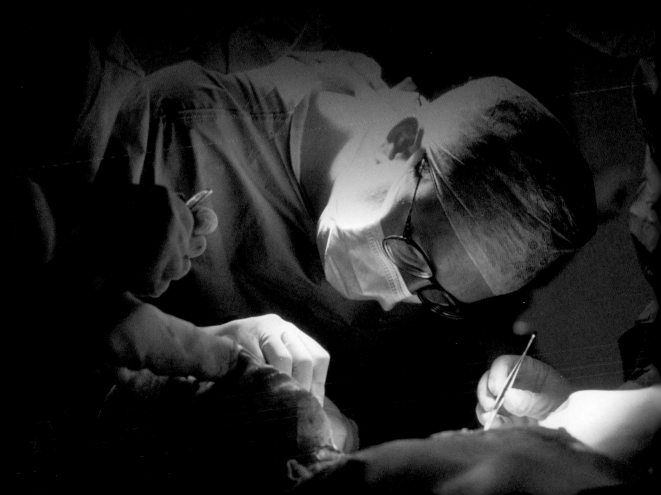

NOTE FROM THE AUTHOR

This book was inspired by an unforgettable friend. While in college, I met a young man who had suffered severe burns as a result of an automobile accident. At first, I was simply stunned by the extent of his injuries and scars because he was still undergoing reconstructive surgery. However, as I got to know him better, I no longer saw anything but the clever, witty man whose friendship I enjoyed. When I interviewed Tony Yarijanian for this book, I asked him to tell me one thing I should be sure to share with readers. He reminded me of my friend when he said, "Tell them, please, don't stare. Burn survivors are more than what you see on the outside." I consider all of the people you'll meet in the Powerful Medicine series heroes—perhaps none more so than those who have survived severe burns.

FOR CURIOUS KIDS EVERYWHERE—THEY'RE THE FUTURE!

Acknowledgments: The author would like to thank the following people for taking the time to share their expertise: Dr. Joseph Banis, Aesthetic and Reconstructive Surgery, Louisville, Kentucky; Dr. Erin Brown, B.C. Professional Firefighters' Burn and Plastic Surgery Unit, Vancouver General Hospital, British Columbia; Dr. Frederick Cahn, CEO BioMedical Strategies; Heidi Cave; Dr. Charles Durfor, Division of General and Resterative Devices, Office of Device Evaluation, Federal Drug Administration; Dr. Peter H. Grossman, Grossman Burn Centers; Larry Hooge, Abbotsford Fire Rescue Service; Dr. John A. Krichbaum, executive director, The American Burn Association; Dr. Jonathan Pascoe, Ilam Medical Centre, Christchurch, New Zealand; Dr. Jeffrey Saffle, University of Utah Burn Center; Dr. Maria Siemionow, Cleveland Clinic; and Tony and Ani Yarijanian. A special thank-you to Skip Jeffery for his loving support during the creative process.

Lerner Publishing Company
A division of Lerner Publishing Group, Inc.
241 First Avenue North
Minneapolis, MN 55401 U.S.A.

Website address: www.lernerbooks.com

Library of Congress Cataloging-in-Publication Data

Markle, Sandra.
    Bad burns / by Sandra Markle.
    p.   cm. — (Powerful medicine)
    Includes bibliographical references and index.
    ISBN 978–0–8225–8702–6 (lib. bdg. : alk. paper)
    1. Burns and scalds—Juvenile literature. 2. Skin—Wounds and injuries—Juvenile literature. 3. Burns and scalds—Treatment—Juvenile literature. I. Title.
RD96.4.M367 2011
617.1'1—dc22   2009034439

Manufactured in the United States of America
1 - DP - 7/15/10

CONTENTS

Most of the time, we don't think about how our bodies keep healthy and active. But if something happens to damage a part, we become very aware of what isn't working properly. **One of those key body parts is our skin.** In this book, you will find dramatic, real-life stories of people who survive severe burns. The stories also tell of the efforts of the doctors and medical researchers who help them. And they show how science and technology make amazing recoveries possible.

MAN SURVIVES EXPLOSION

TONY YARIJANIAN GOT TO WORK EARLY. Tony was the owner of the Safari Tan Salon in Glendale, California. He let himself into the building and switched on the lights and equipment. **Tony had just reached the back of his shop when an explosion shattered the morning quiet and his life.**

Tony said, "There was fire all around me. I was burning and in terrible pain. I ran for the door, but the floor was so slippery I kept falling down."

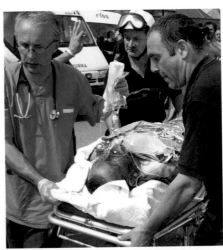

Amazingly—Tony escaped from the fire. Someone yelled at him to drop and roll and he did, crushing out the flames. **But he'd been badly burned.** Within minutes, firefighters and paramedics arrived.

Tony was rushed to the closest hospital with a trauma
center. This is a hospital with twenty-four hour intensive
care specialists on duty and equipment for handling
complex cases. He had severe burns on over 80 percent
of his body.

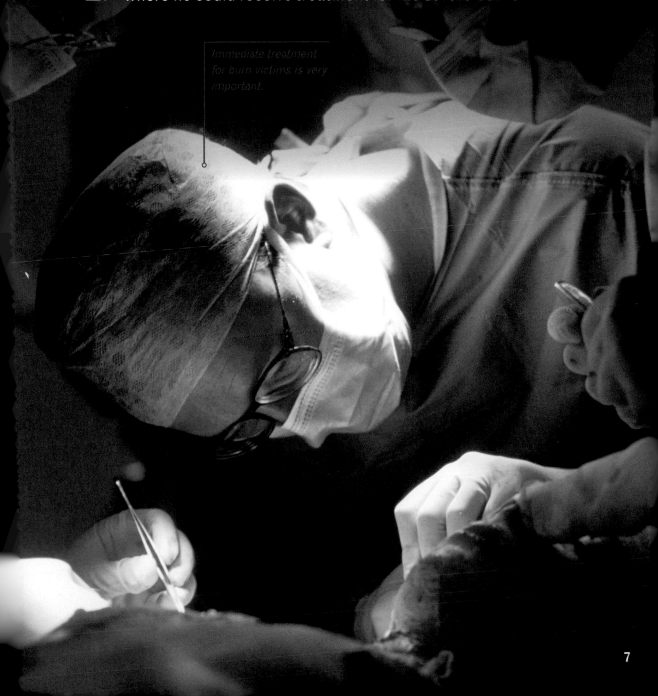

Ani, Tony's wife, said, "When I got to the hospital, I was told four doctors were working on removing his clothes. They had melted onto his body." Tony was quickly transferred to the Grossman Burn Center in Sherman Oaks, California, where he could receive treatment for his severe burns.

Immediate treatment for burn victims is very important.

SKIN IS LIVING ARMOR

SKIN IS ALIVE. It's one of the human body's organs, like the heart and the lungs. In fact, skin is the body's largest organ. It covers every part from scalp to toes. Skin varies in thickness from 0.019 inch (0.5 millimeters) on the eyelids to about 0.15 inch (4 mm) on the palms of the hands and soles of the feet. Human skin gives the body its shape and color, but it does a lot more. Skin protects the body's internal parts from bumps, scrapes, and drying out. It blocks out germs (tiny living things that cause infection and disease). Skin also helps keep the body warm and prevents overheating. Skin is packed with sensors that detect pressure, texture, heat, and pain.

These boys are giving their skin a workout. Luckily, their bodies are constantly producing new skin.

Like the rest of the body, the skin is made up of building blocks called cells. These form two main layers: the epidermis and the dermis.

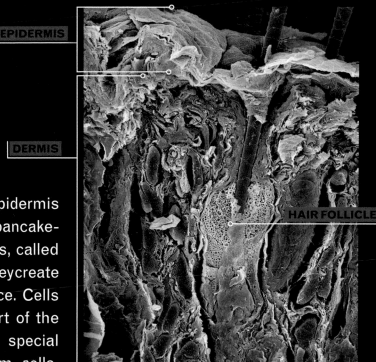

EPIDERMIS

DERMIS

HAIR FOLLICLE

The top of the epidermis is made up of pancake-like layers of cells, called keratinocytes. They create the body's surface. Cells in the lowest part of the epidermis are special cells, called stem cells. They can split and produce new skin cells. The cells of the epidermis are gradually pushed upward by the new cells growing underneath them. When the new cells reach the surface, they die. The dead cells form the body's tough covering. Then they flake off and are replaced by other cells moving to the surface.

The dermis underneath is mainly made up of cells that form an elastic, spongy layer. This layer supports and protects lots of special body parts. These include blood vessels, nerves, and hair follicles (small sacs from which hairs grow). Groups of cells, called glands, give off sweat and the oils that keep the skin soft and elastic. They are also part of the dermis.

Extreme heat or cold, chemicals such as strong acids, or a powerful electric shock can kill the skin's living cells. No matter what causes the damage, skin cell death is called a burn. Burn damage is classified in degrees: first, second, third, and fourth.

First-degree burns, such as mild sunburns, affect only the upper layers of the epidermis. The skin reddens but doesn't blister.

FIRST-DEGREE BURN

Second-degree burns, also called partial thickness burns, damage the epidermis and the upper part of the dermis. The skin blisters, and this may cause minor scarring.

Third-degree burns, also called full thickness burns, damage all the epidermis and some of the dermis. Open wounds form. This may cause major scarring.

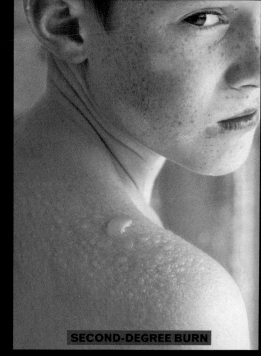

SECOND-DEGREE BURN

THIRD-DEGREE BURN

Most of Tony's wounds were third-degree burns.

WOMAN TRAPPED IN BURNING CAR

FOURTH-DEGREE BURNS ARE SO DEEP THEY EVEN DAMAGE MUSCLES AND BONES. Heidi Cave suffered fourth-degree burns on her legs in a car accident. Her accident happened on a June afternoon in 1998. Heidi was driving her friend to their favorite local coffee shop. Suddenly, a speeding car slammed into the passenger side of Heidi's car. The accident killed Heidi's friend instantly and shoved the car off the road and into a deep valley. The car flipped over and landed about 30 feet (9 meters) below the road. Heidi was still strapped in her seat and hanging upside down. **Before rescuers arrived, fire swept from the car's engine across the top of the wrecked car. This is where Heidi's legs and feet were.**

Fireman Larry Hooge later reported. "We were on the scene within minutes. I was one of the first ones to gear up and go down in the [valley] with the hose line. As soon as we started spraying the car, I heard a woman calling for help. But the car doors were jammed shut. All we could do was douse the fire and get the Jaws of Life (a machine for prying apart crushed and damaged metal) down there to get her out."

Heidi was rushed to the closest hospital with a trauma center.

These firefighters put on gear to protect themselves from burn injuries.

13

Heidi said, "I woke up in the hospital, sobbing. I'd been dreaming, and the pain was so bad I dreamed of being in pain. My boyfriend Scott was there. He said, 'Heidi, do you want to live?' I answered 'Yes!' Then I slipped right back into unconsciousness again."

Over 50 percent of Heidi's body had suffered severe burns. This included most of her body from the chest down. Worse, her legs had suffered fourth-degree burns, damaging her bones. Her legs had to be amputated (cut off).

Doctors use the Rule of Nines to judge how much of the body has suffered second-degree burns or worse. For this rule, the human body is divided into sections. Most—but not all—of these sections represent 9 percent of the whole body. Second-degree burns or worse on 100 percent of the body would be fatal. It's even difficult for people to survive serious burns covering more than one-third of their body. Because they are smaller, infants and young children may be at risk of dying when severe burns cover just 10 percent of their bodies.

RULE OF NINES

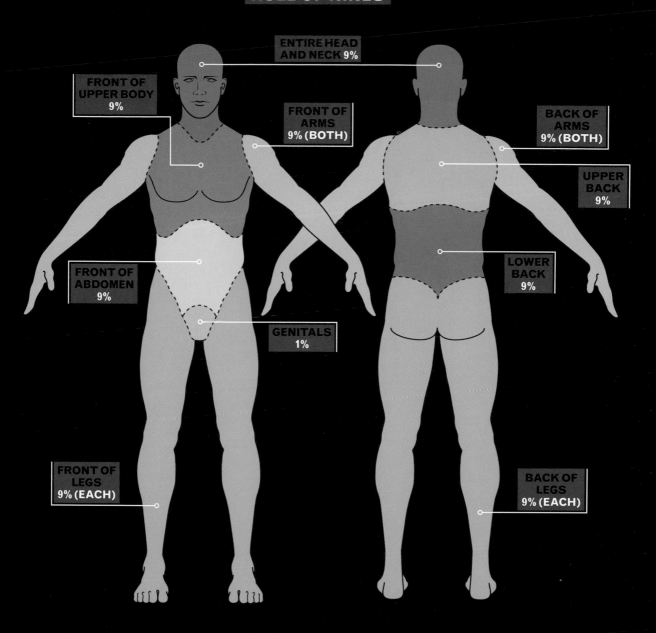

ENTIRE HEAD AND NECK 9%

FRONT OF UPPER BODY 9%

FRONT OF ARMS 9% (BOTH)

FRONT OF ABDOMEN 9%

GENITALS 1%

FRONT OF LEGS 9% (EACH)

BACK OF ARMS 9% (BOTH)

UPPER BACK 9%

LOWER BACK 9%

BACK OF LEGS 9% (EACH)

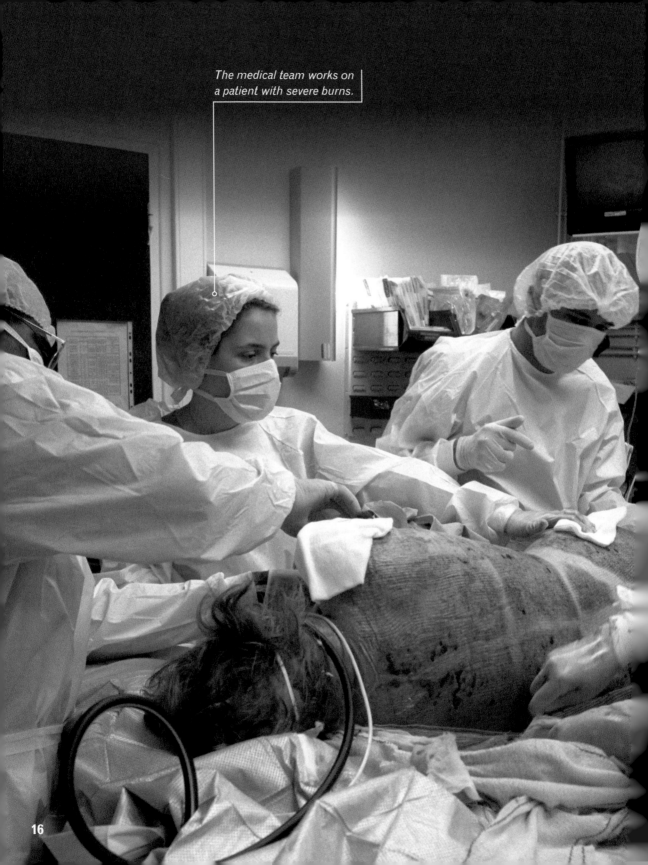

The medical team works on a patient with severe burns.

Doctors use the Rule of Nines when they decide how to treat burns. They also use it to figure out how much body fluid was lost and will need to be replaced.

Severe burns are wounds. With any wound, even a bruise, capillaries (the smallest blood vessels) at the site leak their fluid into the surrounding tissue. Tissue is group of similar cells that work together in the body. The fluid part of the blood is called plasma. The leaking plasma makes an open wound look and feel wet. The wounded area swells.

When a lot of plasma leaks out, the blood flowing through the remainder of the body becomes thicker and slower-moving. It can no longer supply all the oxygen that the heart, the liver, the kidneys, and other vital organs need to work properly. Organs not working can be fatal.

When someone is severely burned, it's important to quickly restore the body's normal fluid level. The doctors insert a needle into one of the patient's veins to supply him or her with a liquid that's similar to the body's own natural fluid. Once the patient's blood flow is restored, the heart can pump normally again.

THE BODY IS FIGHTING INFECTION WHEN PLASMA LEAKS OUT OF CAPILLARIES AT THE WOUND SITE. The plasma is rushing white blood cells to the wound to combat invading germs. There are several different kinds of white blood cells. Some produce special proteins (substances that build body parts). These proteins stick to foreign living things, like germs. Then other kinds of white blood cells are attracted to these proteins. These blood cells surround and destroy the germs. However, the proteins produced by white blood cells can also signal the body's capillaries to leak more plasma into the area. All the extra plasma causes swelling. This buildup of fluid puts pressure on deeper skin tissue. The pressure can kill even more skin cells. Then a second-degree burn can become a third-degree burn.

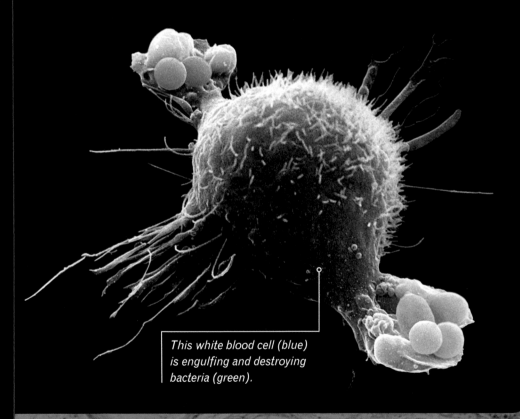

This white blood cell (blue) is engulfing and destroying bacteria (green).

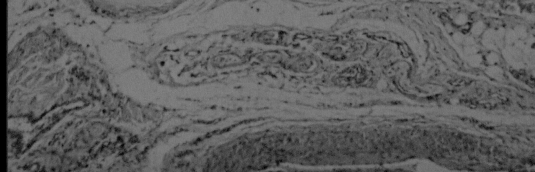

Without any treatment, the human body just naturally closes burn wounds by forming scars. A scar is a tough, thickened line that you can see. The scar formation process can be painful. The scar itself may even limit how freely the scarred area is able to move. Heidi and Tony both had large burn wounds. They needed special treatment to help these wounds heal with as little scarring as possible. Tony's doctor, Peter Grossman, explained. "The key to getting good results when treating severe burns is to get rid of all the dead tissue at the site and very quickly cover the wounds."

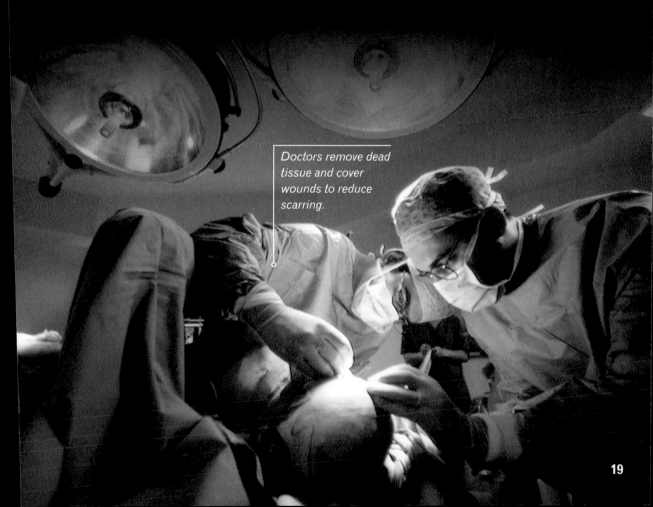

Doctors remove dead tissue and cover wounds to reduce scarring.

REPLACING LOST SKIN

During the operation, Dr. Grossman's team peeled off the dead skin—the layers of skin cells killed by being burned—from his wounds.

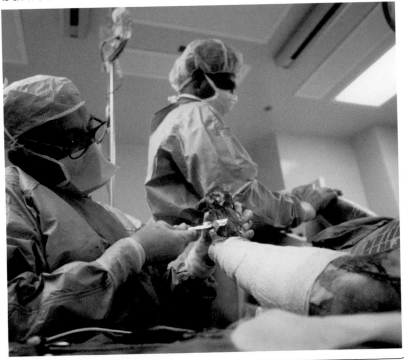

Next, the medical team scrubbed the burn wounds with a brush. This took away any additional dead skin. Then a sanding device was used to remove even more dead skin. This way the layers of skin cells were removed a little bit at a time until blood appeared. The blood is proof the medical team has reached healthy, living skin.

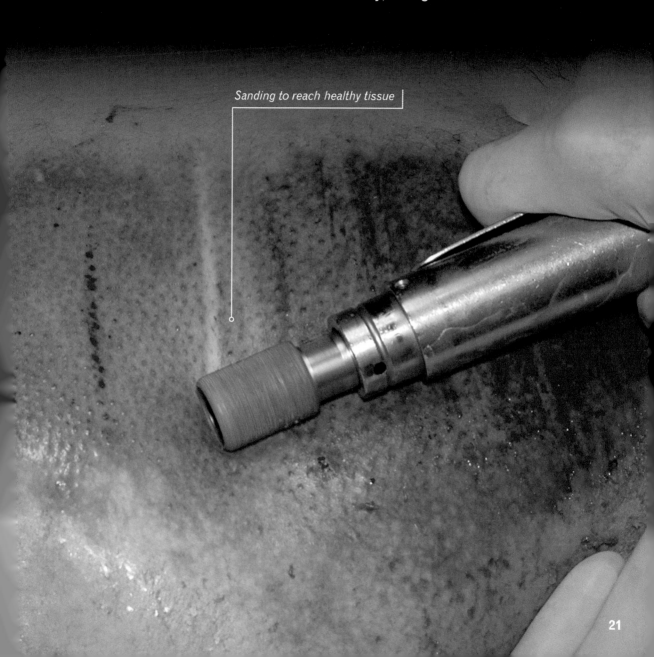

Sanding to reach healthy tissue

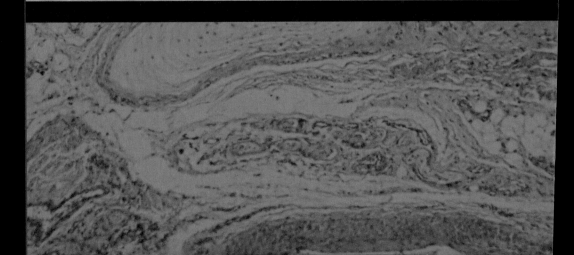

IF YOU'VE EVER HAD A CUT, YOU KNOW THE SKIN SEALS ANY OPEN WOUND. This leaves a scar. The scar, or scar tissue, doesn't just form at the surface. It can form anywhere from the skin's surface to deep inside the body. It can even form on organs, such as the liver or the heart. Normal body tissue is made up of a material called collagen that's like tough gelatin. Scar tissue is also made of this material. But normal tissue is flexible and elastic. Scar tissue is much stiffer. Scar tissue repairs wounds, but it doesn't leave the body exactly as it was. For that reason, doctors treating severe burns work to control and limit scar tissue.

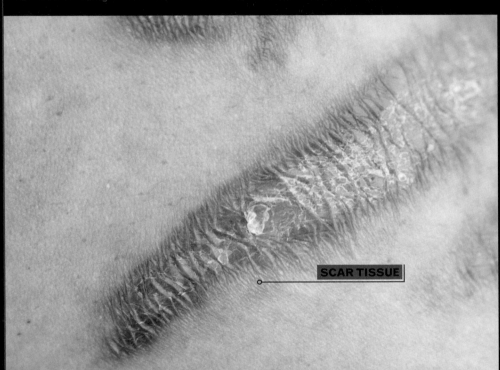

SCAR TISSUE

SCAR TISSUE ALSO TENDS TO CONTRACT. Like zipping up a bulging suitcase, the scar pulls together the edges of healthy skin on either side of the wound. If scarring happens around joints, like fingers, elbows, and knees, that body part may become stiff. Sometimes scar tissue keeps on growing. It piles up layer upon layer beyond the wounded area. Such out-of-control scar growth forms keloid scars.

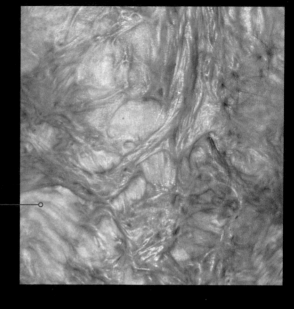

Besides being uncomfortable, keloid scars can affect a person's appearance and how they feel about themselves.

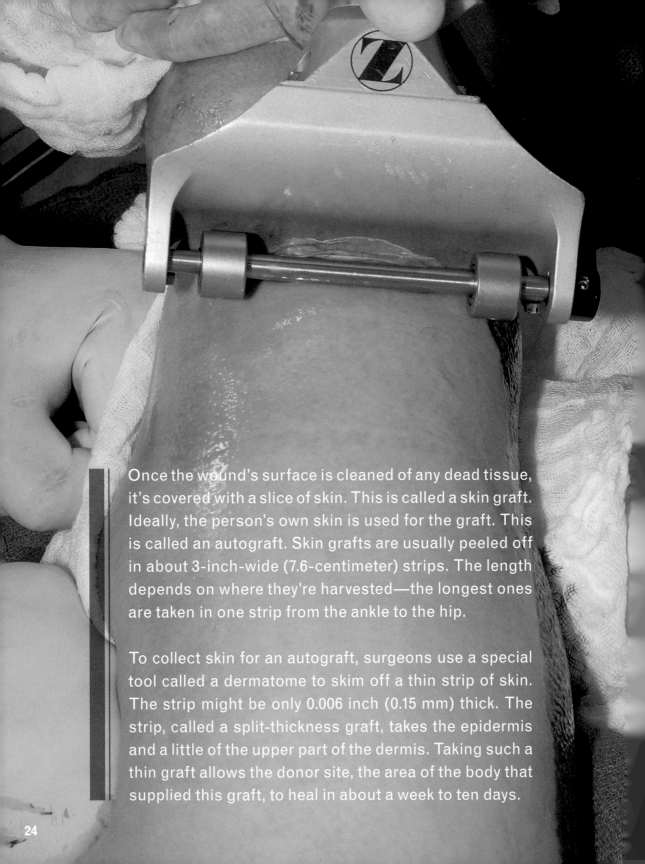

Once the wound's surface is cleaned of any dead tissue, it's covered with a slice of skin. This is called a skin graft. Ideally, the person's own skin is used for the graft. This is called an autograft. Skin grafts are usually peeled off in about 3-inch-wide (7.6-centimeter) strips. The length depends on where they're harvested—the longest ones are taken in one strip from the ankle to the hip.

To collect skin for an autograft, surgeons use a special tool called a dermatome to skim off a thin strip of skin. The strip might be only 0.006 inch (0.15 mm) thick. The strip, called a split-thickness graft, takes the epidermis and a little of the upper part of the dermis. Taking such a thin graft allows the donor site, the area of the body that supplied this graft, to heal in about a week to ten days.

After the skin graft is peeled off the donor site, it's put through a mesher. This machine pokes the skin full of holes so its structure is like a fine fishnet. This means the autograft can be spread over a larger area of the wound. The holes also let the fluid that leaks out of the cleaned wound escape outside the body.

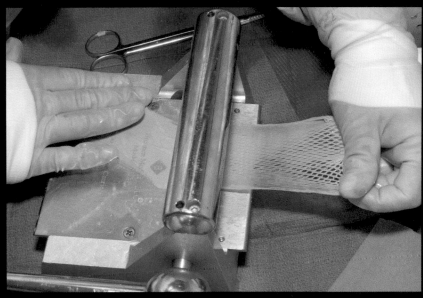

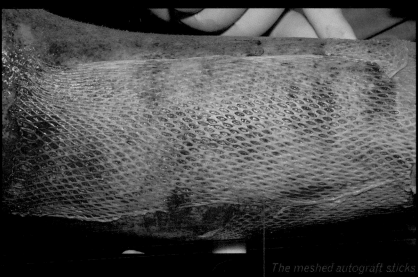

The meshed autograft sticks to the cleaned wound.

However, patients like Tony and Heidi may not have enough healthy skin left to only have autografts. Then they also have to have allografts. These are slices of skin removed from someone who has died. This person donated skin to help someone else just as people donate their hearts, kidneys, and other organs.

Heidi's burn treatment specialist, Dr. Erin Brown, explained. "Allografts help block out bacteria and [limit] scar tissue formation. Because they're foreign to the body, they'll never grow, but they make great biological Band-Aids. Allografts also give the areas that have been harvested for autografts on the patient's body time to heal. Then the donor sites can be harvested again."

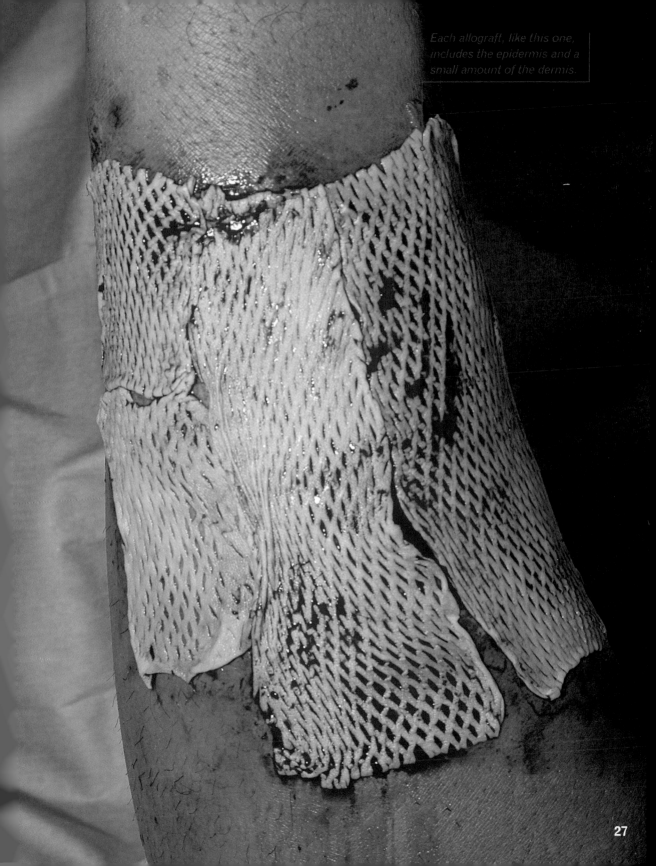

Each allograft, like this one, includes the epidermis and a small amount of the dermis.

The skin graft sticks to the cleaned wound like a paper tissue pressed over wet skin. The graft must stay in contact with the cleaned wound for blood vessels to grow into the graft. Then the graft will become a permanent and healthy part of the body's skin. If the wound leaks a lot of fluid, it could lift the graft. To help keep the graft pressed against the wound, doctors may suture (stitch) or staple the graft in place. Then the graft is covered with a dressing that keeps it clean without sticking to it.

Heidi said, "I had over twenty surgeries my first year to perform skin grafts—most of those during the first seven months after my accident. They seemed to be so slow to heal. Once I had to lie on my stomach for five days to help my backside heal."

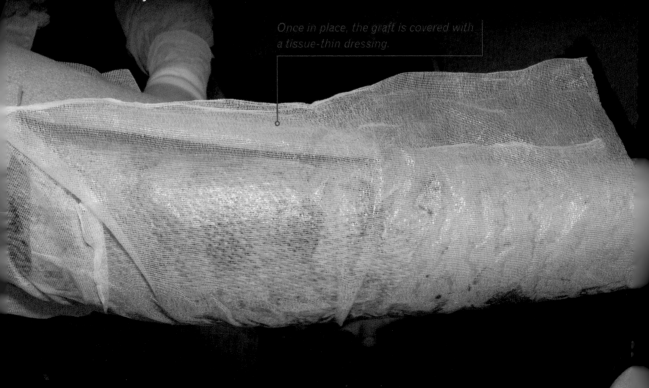

Once in place, the graft is covered with a tissue-thin dressing.

DR. GROSSMAN SAID, "WE'VE DISCOVERED YET ANOTHER WAY TO ATTACH SKIN GRAFTS — GLUING THEM DOWN. We make the graft slightly larger than the wound. Then we apply the glue, like caulk, sealing the edges. The glue is similar to Super Glue and Krazy Glue. Applying it is so **much** faster than using either sutures or staples. It lets us work on more burn areas during a single surgery than we otherwise could. The glue eventually breaks down into bits that can be washed away. By then, the graft is permanently attached."

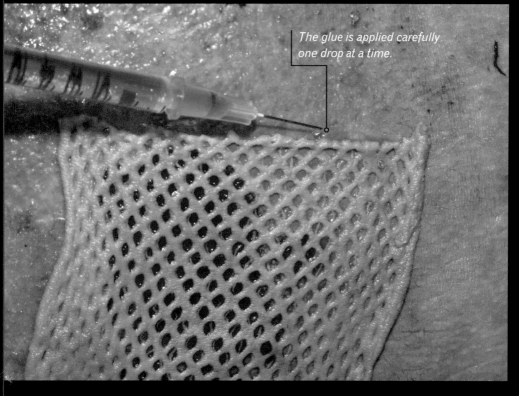

The glue is applied carefully one drop at a time.

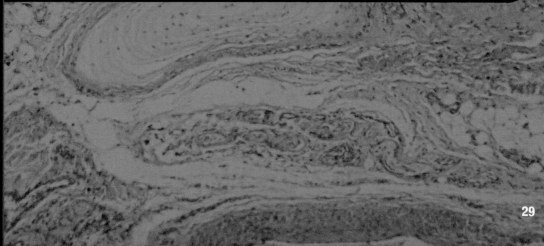

Both Tony Yarijanian and Heidi Cave were hospitalized for about three months during the skin-grafting process. That wasn't the end of their treatment. Both spent time in physical therapy doing exercises to help their body flex and move normally. Like this boy *(right)*, both also needed to wear pressure garments, special snug-fitting elastic suits. Dr. Grossman explained. "The goal is to continually apply pressure to the scars. We've learned that this helps the scars flatten out and usually keeps them from overhealing [building up and spreading out beyond the wounded area]."

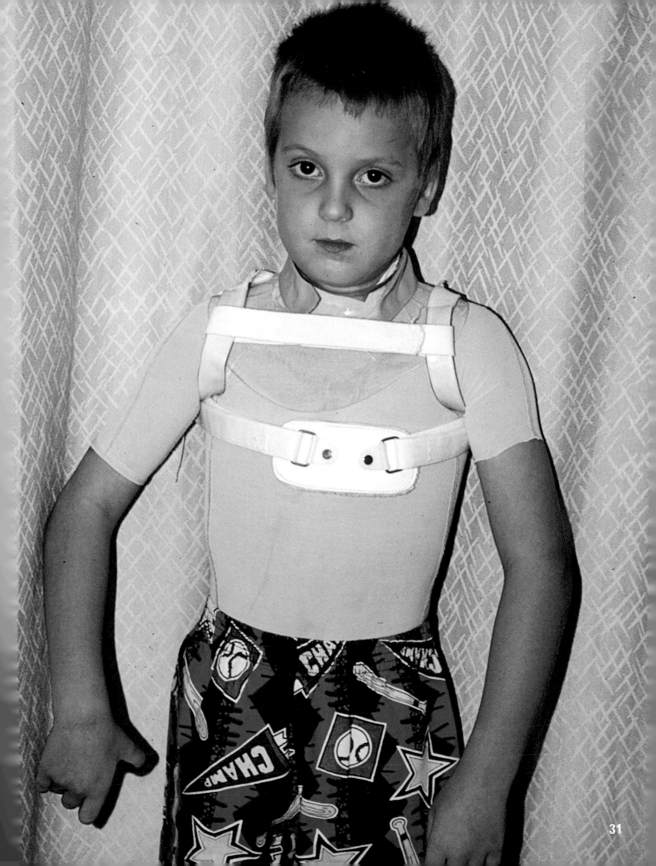

Tony said, "The most amazing grafting was on my face. They had to graft skin over almost my entire face."

Dr. Grossman said, "The key to the success we had was that we were very aggressive in removing unhealthy tissue and using allografts as biological dressings. This way we kept down the risk of infection. We also reserved the very best autografts for Tony's face. However, even with all of this, I'm still amazed at the results, considering how he looked when he came in."

Heidi said, "Grafted skin is better than scar tissue, but it isn't the same as normal skin. My sense of touch is duller where I was grafted, and there are no sweat glands, so I overheat easily. I also have to be super careful to avoid getting sunburned. Our skin is our largest organ, and it protects our bodies, but we need to take care of it. Mine has had a hard time, so I have to be extra careful."

This is Tony after his successful skin-grafting surgeries.

33

NEW SKIN
TECHNIQUES

RESEARCHERS HAVE FOUND A WAY TO GROW SKIN IN A LABORATORY. First, they remove a postage-stamp-sized slice of healthy epidermis from the patient's body. Then they provide a mesh framework for the skin cells. The cells split and grow rapidly on this supporting framework. In about three weeks, the postage-stamp-sized slice of skin becomes postcard-sized. That's big enough to be an effective autograft.

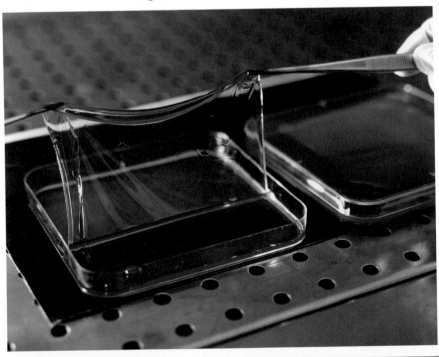

There isn't always enough donated human skin available for allografts. So researchers have developed a number of artificial skin products. One of these is Integra, a two-layer graft material. It is made up of a collagen spongelike material (produced from cow collagen) topped with a protective coating. The spongelike layer fills in the gap left in the skin when the dermis was destroyed. It gives the damaged area a more natural shape. Blood vessels grow up into this gap, and the artificial skin becomes attached to the wound. After a few weeks, the protective layer is removed and topped with a very thin autograft of the patient's epidermal cells.

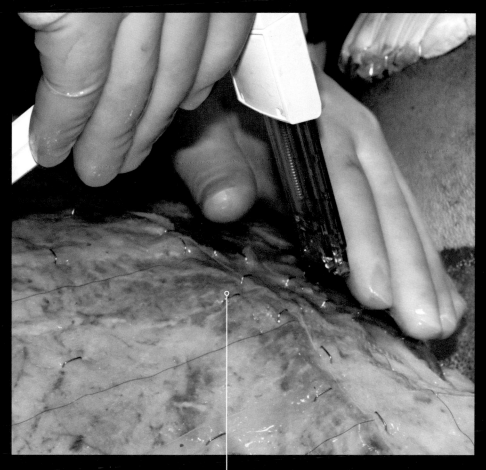

A doctor attaches artificial skin to a burn victim's back.

In the future, people who suffer severe burns may not need grafts. In 2008 Dr. Joerg Gerlach began testing a new system to regrow skin. First, researchers collect a sample of the patient's healthy skin. Next, they process this sample to remove the skin's stem cells. The scientists load the stem cells into a sterile (absolutely clean) spray gun and spray them as a fine mist over the burn wound. They cover the wound with a dressing to which tubes are connected. These tubes contain a fluid with antibiotics to fight infection and chemicals to help the stem cells reproduce. This system could cover large wounds quickly and greatly reduce scar tissue.

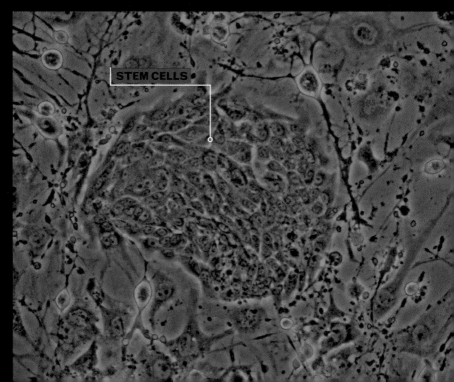

A fine mist of stem cells is being sprayed over a burn wound.

COLD BURNS

FREEZING COLD IS THE OPPOSITE OF FIERY HEAT, BUT THE EFFECT ON THE SKIN IS THE SAME—SKIN DAMAGE.

Skin damaged by freezing is called frostbite. Like a heat burn, it's measured in degrees: first, second, and third. People who have suffered third-degree frostbite to fingers and toes often have damaged these parts beyond repair. Infection sets in, and the parts have to be amputated. Dr. Jeffrey Saffle explains. **"Frostbite damages the lining of the blood vessels, causing lots of little blood clots to form.** That blocks blood flow through small vessels. This is especially a problem for fingers and toes."

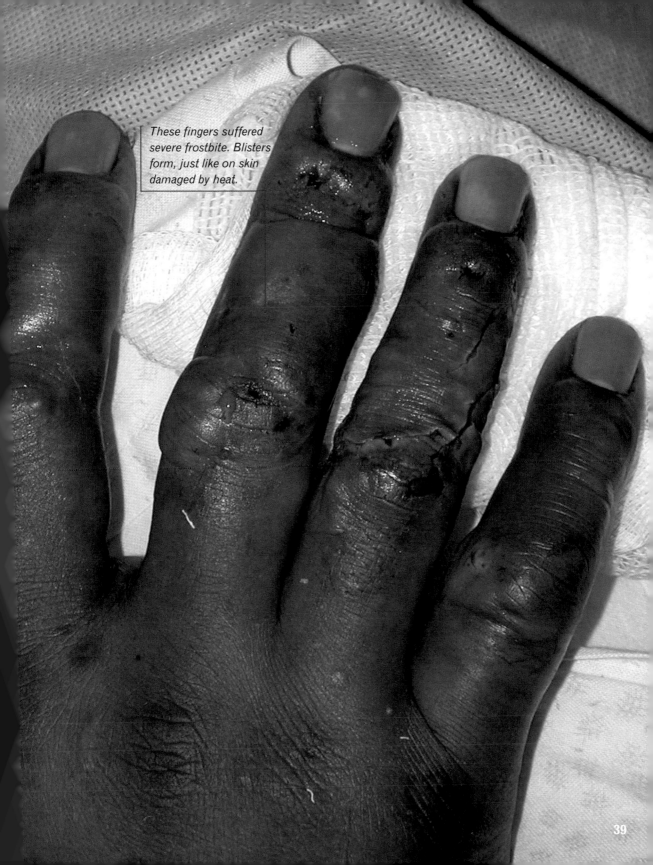

These fingers suffered severe frostbite. Blisters form, just like on skin damaged by heat.

A new treatment is giving frostbite sufferers new hope. The treatment is an injection of tissue plasminogen activator (tPA). This chemical breaks down the clots caused by frostbite and restores blood flow to the area. If blood flow can start before much skin tissue dies, the body part can be saved. To see what a difference tPA makes, compare *(facing page)* the X-rays of this frostbite victim's left hand before treatment and about twelve hours later. The fingers appear to have lots more blood vessels after treatment because blood is again flowing through them.

So far many, though not all, of the patients who have received tPA treatment have recovered without suffering any amputations. To know for certain if it's the tPA treatment that makes the difference, scientists need to compare the results in people who receive the drug to those who don't. But as Dr. Saffle said, "When we know tPA can help, how can we deny anyone treatment?"

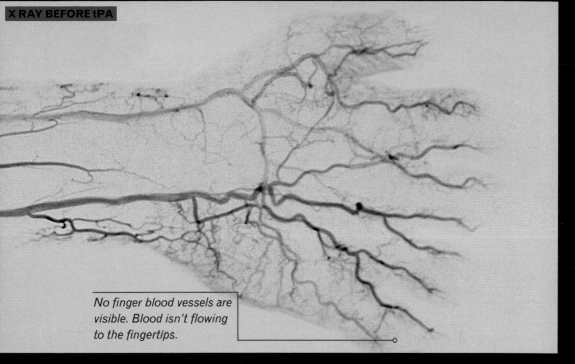

No finger blood vessels are visible. Blood isn't flowing to the fingertips.

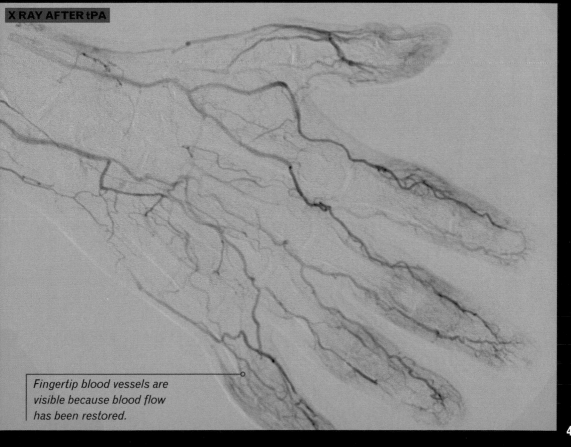

Fingertip blood vessels are visible because blood flow has been restored.

41

UPDATES

TONY YARIJANIAN works as a network engineer. He also enjoys spending time in the gym and with his wife and two children. **HEIDI CAVE** married her boyfriend Scott, and they have two children. She volunteers for the local professional firefighters' burn fund and the International Association of Burn Camps. These are camps where children who are burn survivors can have fun and make friends with other burn survivors. Like Tony, she leads a full life. So do the thousands of others who have survived severe burns. Medical research, engineering, and technology are enabling doctors to restore the damage caused by serious burns in ways that could once only be imagined.

TONY AND ANI YARIJANIAN

HEIDI CAVE

43

BE FIRE SAFE

- The American Burn Association estimates that more than fifty thousand people in the United States alone are hospitalized each year for burn treatment. Even more shocking is the fact that as many as five thousand people in the United States die annually from severe burns. Here are tips that will help you protect your skin from burns and keep you healthy. Be sure you know what number to call to reach emergency services in case of a fire.

- Work with an adult to plan an escape route from every room of your home in case of fire. Plan what to do if your normal escape route is blocked by flames.

- Be sure your home has smoke detectors. Remind an adult to check the batteries in them the first week of every month.

- Be careful not to get close to the stove when food is cooking. Hot liquids and food can burn skin too.

- Stay away from outdoor power lines. Never climb on power poles. Never fly a kite near them.

- If your clothes catch on fire, stop, drop, and roll on the floor or ground. Then get help at once. Do not remove clothes that could be stuck to burn-damaged skin.

SKIN IS AMAZING!

- Your skin cools you off. As your body heats up, the skin's blood vessels dilate, or open wider, letting more blood flow through to carry away heat. The skin's sweat glands also pour out sweat. As the sweat evaporates, or dries, it uses up some body heat too— another cooling effect.

- Your skin helps keep you warm. As your body cools down, the skin's blood vessels constrict, or reduce how wide they're open. That limits blood flow and the amount of heat leaving your body. Sweat glands stop producing sweat, and tiny muscles pull the skin's hair erect. These hairs help trap body heat close to the skin.

- Skin makes up about one-sixth of your total body weight. It is the fastest-growing part of your body. It keeps renewing itself throughout your life. Cells at the bottom of the epidermis continue to grow and produce more skin cells. Dead cells at the surface of the epidermis are shed or rubbed off every day.

GLOSSARY

allograft: a graft of skin transferred from another person

autograft: a graft of the person's own skin

bacteria: tiny, single-celled living things. Some are helpful, and other can cause diseases.

cell: the smallest unit of life

dermatome: an instrument for cutting thin slices of skin for skin grafts

dermis: the inner layer of skin. It contains sweat glands; nerves; blood vessels; and hair follicles, the living part of the hair.

epidermis: the outer layer of skin. It is made up of stacked layers of cells. The base layer is made up of living cells that split and produce new cells. The surface is a protective coat of dead cells.

full-thickness burn: another name for a third-degree burn, one that destroys both the epidermis and the dermis

mesher: an instrument designed to expand skin to be used in a skin graft

partial-thickness burn: another name for second-degree burns, ones that damage the epidermis and may also cause some damage to the upper part of the dermis

plasma: the fluid part of blood

scar: tough, stiff tissue that forms filling in a wound

skin graft: skin that is transferred from one area of the body or another body to cover an open wound, such as a severe burn causes

stem cells: cells that reproduce and form more cells. Stem cells also have the ability to change the kinds of cells they produce and the kinds of tissues they will form.

tissue: group of similar cells that work together in the body

MORE INFORMATION

Want to learn more information about the skin and the latest medical advancements for treating burns? Check these resources.

BOOKS

Cobb,Vicki. *Your Body Battles a Skinned Knee.* Minneapolis: Millbrook Press, 2009. Micrographs and cartoons explain how skin cells battle germs and how they help heal a wound.

Donovan, Sandy. *Stay Clear: What You Should Know About Skin Care.* Minneapolis: Lerner Publications Company, 2009. This book gives advice on how to take care of your skin, along with an overview of what skin is and what is does.

Johnson, Rebecca L. *Ultra-Organized Cell Systems.* Minneapolis: Millbrook Press, 2008. Clear simple text, exact medical drawings, and humorous art explain how cells organize into tissue, organs, and organ systems.

Klosterman, Lorrie. *Skin.* New York: Benchmark Books, 2008. Investigate your skin, and explore what it does for your body.

Lew, Kristi. *Itch & Ooze.* Minneapolis: Millbrook Press, 2009. This is a humorous look at the amazing human skin and the many things that can go wrong and right with it.

Markle, Sandra. *Outside and Inside You.* New York: Scholastic,1991. See microscopic views of the skin's surface, and look even deeper to view its structure. Discover why your skin is so important to the rest of your body.

Silverstein, Alvin, Virginia Silverstein, and Laura Silverstein Nunn. *Burns and Blisters.* Danbury, CT: Franklin Watts, 2002. Learn more about how a burn damages the skin and the treatment of this injury. The emphasis is on how to avoid burns.

WEBSITES

McGruff's Fire Safety Game
http://www.mcgruff.org/Games/fs.php
Play this animated game to practice fire safety.

Smokey for Kids
http://www.smokeybear.com/kids/default.asp
Play games and learn about fire safety with Smokey the Bear.

SELECTED BIBLIOGRAPHY

NEWSPAPERS

Schaffer, Amanda "Cadaver Skin Fills the Gap in Burn Cases." *New York Times*. February 5, 2006. http://www.nytimes.com/2006/05/02/health/02skin.html (May 12, 2010).

WEBSITES

Bourzac, Katherine. "Faster-Healing Artificial Skin." *Technology Review*. April 30, 2007. http://www.technologyreview.com/Biotech/18601/ (September 15, 2008).

"The Burn Resource Center." Burn Survivor Resource Center. N.d. http://www.burnsurvivor.com/ (September 15, 2008).

"Clot-Dissolving Agent May Be Beneficial in Treatment of Severe Frostbite." *Science Daily*. June 19, 2007. http://www.sciencedaily.com/releases/2007/06/070618164146.htm (September 15, 2008).

"Epicel™ Wins Marketing Approval for Severe Burn Victims." *Bio-Medicine*. October 29, 2007. http://www.bio-medicine.org/medicine-news-1/Epicel-28TM-29-Wins-Marketing-Approval-for-Severe-Burn-Victims-4928-2/ (September 15, 2008).

Regenerative Therapy for Epidermal Burns: Are Stem Cells the Answer. *Rice University*. N.d. http://www.owlnet.rice.edu/~bioc341/Proj_to_post/G19.pdf (September 15, 2008).

University at Buffalo. "Genetically Engineered Skin Substitute Is Designed to Promote Wound Healing." *ScienceDaily*. April 4, 2001. http://www.sciencedaily.com/releases/2001/04/010402073217.htm (September 15, 2008).

University of Pittsburgh. "Burn Therapy: A Regenerative Approach." McGowan Institute for Regenerative Medicine. N.d. http://www.mirm.pitt.edu/news/article.asp?qEmpID=328 (September 15, 2008).

TELEPHONE INTERVIEWS

Banis, Joseph, August 22, 2008.

Brown, Erin, August 29, 2008.

Cahn, Frederick, August 7, 2008.

Cave, Heidi, August 2, 2008.

Durfor, Charles, August 7, 2008.

Grossman, Peter, August 14, 2008.

Hooge, Larry, August 6, 2008.

Saffle, Jeffrey, August 20, 2008.

Siemionow, Maria, August 28, 2008.

Yarijanian, Ani, August 6, 2008.

Yarijanian, Tony, August 6, 2008.

INDEX

PHOTO CREDITS

Some of the images in this book simulate events that happened and are not actual photographs of the events taken at the time they occurred.
The images in this book are used with the permission of: © Philippe Eranian/Sygma/CORBIS, pp. 1, 7, 19; © Image Source/Getty Images, (all backgrounds) pp. 3, 8, 18, 22, 29, 44, 45, 46, 47, 48; © Reuters/CORBIS, p. 4; © Comstock/Photolibrary, pp. 4-5; © Gabe Palmer/CORBIS, p. 6; © Ed Bock/Surf/CORBIS, p. 8; © Steve Gschmeissner/Photo Researchers, Inc., p. 9; © age fotostock/SuperStock, p. 10; © Mike Berceanu/ Photolibrary, p. 11 (top); © St. Stephen's Hospital, London/Photo Researchers, Inc., p. 11 (bottom); © DesignPics Inc./Photolibrary, pp. 12-13; © Laura Westlund/Independent Picture Service, p. 15; © Dung Vo Trung/Sygma/CORBIS, pp. 16-17; © Dr. David Phillips/Visuals Unlimited, Inc., p. 18; © JP Laffont/ Sygma/CORBIS, p. 20; Photos courtesy of Alan Goldstein and Alan Zuckerman, Grossman Burn Center, pp. 20-21, 24, 25 (both), 27, 28, 29, 31; © Joti/Science Photo Library/Photo Researchers, Inc., p. 22; © Dr. P. Marazzi/Photo Researchers, Inc., p. 23; Photos courtesy of the Yarijanian Family, pp. 33, 43 (top); © Klaus Guldbrandsen/Science Photo Library/Photo Researchers, Inc., p. 34; © Barry Slaven/The Medical File/ Peter Arnold, Inc., p. 35; © Jennifer Waters/Photo Researchers, Inc., p. 36; © James King-Holmes/Photo Researchers, Inc., p. 37; Photos courtesy of Dr. Jeffrey Saffle, pp. 38-39, 41 (both); Photo courtesy of the Cave Family, p. 43 (bottom).

Front cover: © Dr. David Phillips/Visuals Unlimited, Inc. Back cover: © Image Source/Getty Images.